P9-CWE-162

ANSEL ADAMS

Photographs

WINGS BOOKS

New York • Avenel, New Jersey

Copyright © 1992 by Outlet Book Company, Inc.

All rights reserved.

Published by Wings Books,
distributed by Outlet Book Company, Inc.,
a Random House Company,
40 Engelhard Avenue, Avenel, New Jersey, 07001.

Grateful acknowledgement is made to The National Archives and the Bettman
Archives for permission to use their prints of the artwork.

Printed and bound in Singapore

Library of Congress Cataloging-in-Publication Data

Adams, Ansel, 1902–1984
    Ansel Adams.
        p.   cm.
    ISBN 0-517-07763-9
    1. Photography, Artistic.   I. Title.
TR654.A32   1992
779′.092—dc20

                                                    92-987
                                                    CIP

8   7   6   5   4   3   2   1

Some photographers take reality...and impose the domination of their own thought and spirit. Others come before reality more tenderly and a photograph to them is an instrument of love and revelation.

—ANSEL ADAMS

1. In Glacier National Park

2. Grand Teton

3. Rocky Mountain National Park, Never Summer Range

4. Rock of Ages, Big Room, Carlsbad Caverns National Park

5. Saguaros, Saguaro National Monument

6. From Logan Pass, Glacier National Park

7. Grand Teton

8. Grand Canyon National Park

9. Canyon de Chelly

10. Church, Taos Pueblo, New Mexico 1941

11. Navaho Girl, Canyon de Chelly, Arizona

12. Grand Canyon National Park

3. Jupiter Terrace–Fountain Geyser Pool, Yellowstone National Park

14. Grand Canyon National Park

15. In Glacier National Park

16. In Glacier National Park

17. Court of the Patriarchs, Zion National Park

18. Untitled

19. In Saguaro National Monument

20. In Glacier National Park

21. Church, Taos Pueblo, New Mexico 1942

22. Navaho Woman and Infant, Canyon de Chelly, Arizona

23. Dance, San Ildefonso Pueblo, New Mexico 1942

24. Canyon de Chelly

25. In Rocky Mountain National Park

26. Fountain Geyser Pool, Yellowstone National Park

27. Old Faithful Geyser, Yellowstone National Park

28. Half Dome, Apple Orchard, Yosemite

9. Moraine, Rocky Mountain National Park

30. Kearsage Pinnacles

31. Formations, along trail in the Big Room, beyond the Temple of the Sun

32. Heaven's Peak

Afterword

To photograph truthfully and effectively is to see beneath the surfaces and record the qualities of nature and humanity which live or are latent in all things.[1]

Born in San Francisco in 1902, Ansel Adams came of age as a photographer during the Great Depression. At a time when "environment" meant little more than dust bowls, hurricanes, and crop failure to most people, Adams focused his interest on the natural world and man's relation to it:

Here are worlds of experience beyond the world of the aggressive man, beyond history, and beyond science. The moods and qualities of nature and the revelations of great art are equally difficult to define; we can grasp them only in the depths of our perceptive spirit.[2]

For more than 50 years, in his photographs of the wilderness, his writings, and his participation in the Sierra Club and other conservation groups, Adams dedicated himself to the preservation of America's natural beauty.

Adams's love of the wilderness began when a family trip to Yosemite National Park in 1916 awakened him to the beauty of the

Sierra Nevada Mountains. In 1920, after a short stint working at a photo-finishing company in San Francisco, Adams took a job as a custodian at the headquarters of the Sierra Club at Yosemite and soon became a guide, leading many Sierra Club outings. He explored the mountains, camera in hand, throughout the 1920s, taking hundreds of photographs and progressing quickly from the "soft-focus" style of traditional landscape photography to the more direct style for which he is now famous.

Adams spent much time during this period in Santa Fe and Taos, where he met and became friends with Alfred Stieglitz, Georgia O'Keeffe, Mary Austin, and others in the small arts community developing there. He collaborated with Mary Austin on *Taos Pueblo*, a book published in 1930 that depicts in prose and photographs a deep love and understanding of the Southwest. In 1950, Adams's photographs of the Sierra Nevada and Owens River Valley were used to illustrate an edition of Austin's classic *The Land of Little Rain*.

A meeting with Paul Strand in Taos in 1930 opened Adams's eyes to the extraordinary possibilities of photography as an art form. An accomplished pianist, Adams had considered a career in music. Yet the austere beauty and technical perfection of Strand's work convinced Adams that his future lay in the art of the camera:

> I tried to keep both arts alive, but the camera won. I found that while the camera does not express the soul, perhaps a photograph can![3]

In 1932, Adams, Edward Weston, Imogen Cunningham, and other young photographers established Group f/64, organized as a reaction against conventional pictorial photography. Their goal was to emulate Stieglitz's breakthrough "straight" approach, to produce photographs like those described by *Photo-Miniature* in a 1921 review of a Stieglitz exhibition:

> You have the subject itself, as revealed by the natural play of light and shade about it, without disguise or attempt at interpretation, simply set forth with perfect technique.[4]

In 1933, Adams brought his photographs to Stieglitz in New York City. Three years later, Stieglitz put on an exhibition of Adams's photographs at his renowned gallery, An American Place. Stieglitz's interest and praise encouraged Adams; Stieglitz's belief that "art is the affirmation of life," would serve as Adams's guiding principle for the rest of his life.[5]

Adams and his wife Virginia moved to Yosemite in 1936, taking over her father's photography studio there. During the war, Adams performed a great deal of civilian work for the government. One such project involved photographing the Manzanar War Relocation Camp in Owens Valley, California; the results of his work were published in 1944 in *Born Free and Equal*. As the official photographer for the Mural Project, Adams traveled throughout the American West taking pictures at Indian reservations and national parks under the auspices of the Department of Interior. Two Guggenheim Fellowships allowed him to continue his travels when the Mural Project was abandoned, and by 1950, Adams had traveled as far as Alaska, a wilderness that awed him and reaffirmed his devotion to conservation.

Throughout the 1950s Ansel Adams produced photographs at an almost astonishing rate: he published eight books, including his *Basic Photo Series*, a highly respected work on techniques and technical matters. He and Minor White funded the prestigious magazine *Aperture*. Adams also worked with Dorothea Lange on a *Life* magazine feature on the Mormons of Utah. Returning to California in 1962, Adams helped establish The Friends of Photography, a non-profit organization that offered educational programs and mounted photographic exhibitions throughout the world. With equal conviction Adams energetically pursued the cause of conservation. He served on the board of directors of the Sierra Club for 37 years; he lobbied in both the private and public sectors, urging companies like Pacific Gas and Electric and presidents Ford, Carter, and Reagan to develop sound environmental policies.

Ansel Adams died in April 1984. His spirit lives on in the more than 100,000 acres of the Sierra designated the Ansel Adams Wilderness Area; in Mt. Ansel Adams, an 11,760-foot peak in Yosemite National Park; and especially through the legacy of his photographs, which offer a rare perception of the American wilderness.

In describing the particular quality of Adams's photographs, John Szarkowski reminds us of Adams's training as a musician:

> To describe in a small monochrome picture the difference between the twilight of early morning and that of evening...requires that every tone of the gray scale be tuned to a precise relationship of pitch and volume so that the picture as a whole sounds a chord...[6]

For Adams, control over the total process of picture-making was as integral to his art as the control a musician has over his instrument.[7] It began at the moment Adams selected his subject. He had the ability to visualize precisely the image he wanted to capture, practicing an "intuitive search for meaning, shape, form, texture, and the projection of the image-format on the subject."[8]

Adams was also a master of the technical aspects of photography.

He used a now-famous musical metaphor in explaining why he was involved each step of the way: "the negative is comparable to the composer's score and the print to its performance."[9] Adams printed his own negatives and directly supervised the content and quality of all his published works.

While teaching at the Art Center in Los Angeles in 1940, Adams worked out a precise method of coordinating the actual light on the subject to be photographed, exposure, and developing so that the photographer's vision would be faithfully preserved. His system, based on assigning values from zero to nine to every tone between black and white, took the "guesswork" out of photography. This method freed the photographer to concentrate on the creative, to capture, as Adams wrote in his introduction to *Portfolio Three*, "a moment of wonder."

> Both the grand and the intimate aspects of nature can be revealed in the expressive photograph. Both can stir enduring affirmations and discoveries, and can surely help the spectator in his search for identification with the vast world of natural beauty and the wonder surrounding him.[10]

This identification with the world of natural beauty informs all of Adams's work; he described his own feeling about the Sierra as an "almost symbiotic relationship."[11] For Adams, it was the details, the changing moods and reality of the Sierra—indeed, of any of his subjects—that attracted the eye and the imagination; his photographs were not meant to mirror facts, but rather "to present visual evidences of memories and mysteries at a personal level of experience."[12]

The unusual sharpness and clarity of the light of the high mountains brought forth photographs of dramatic contrast and texture. In the vast, unpeopled, sun-drenched vistas of the Southwest, Adams found "a diversity of geographic forms, the ever-changing light and almost primordial force of the desert."[13] Although he is best known for grand scale photographs, Adams resisted being classified solely as a landscape photographer. Close-ups of such subjects as ferns and leaves (plates 16 and 20), taken partly as an experiment at Glacier National Park, reflect his attention to detail and lighting, his interest in "the intimate aspects of nature." His picture of Old Faithful (plate 27) conveys the exuberance he experienced at one of his favorite sites. In the almost sensual photographs of cacti in the Southwest (plates 5 and 19), another of Adams's principles is apparent:

> Some photographers take reality...and upon it impose the domination of their own thought and spirit. Others come before reality more tenderly and a photograph to them is an instrument of love and revelation.[14]

In his photographs of Native Americans (plates 11, 22, and 23) and buildings (plates 10 and 21) in the Southwest, man and his creations are seen within a larger context; in the portraits of a people tied through time to the land, of buildings which seem to rise almost organically from the landscape, Adams confirms that man is an integral part of nature.

In 1963, in his introduction to *What a Majestic World (Portfolio Four)*, Adams wrote:

> In some [photographs] the essences of light and space dominate; in others, the substance of rock and wood, and the luminous insistence of growing things....It is my intention to present—through the medium of photography—intuitive observations of the natural world which may have meaning to spectators...[15]

That Ansel Adams succeeded, as few other photographers have, in presenting his feelings and perceptions to a wide audience is evident in the continuing popularity of his books and exhibitions of his work. Ansel Adams's emphasis on finding an ideal reality and a *personal* significance in the wonders of nature, and his intense and unceasing activism in support of conservation, celebrate an America—and a spirit—well worth revisiting.

NOTES

1. Ansel Adams, *The Portfolios of Ansel Adams* (Boston: Little, Brown, and Company), Introduction to *Portfolio One*
2. Ibid., Introduction to *Portfolio Three*
3. Ansel Adams, *Yosemite and the Range of Light* (Boston: Little, Brown and Company), 12
4. Beaumont Newhall, *The History of Photography* (New York: The Museum of Modern Art), 113
5. Barry Pritzker, *Ansel Adams* (New York: Crescent Books), 13
6. *The Portfolios of Ansel Adams*, viii
7. *The History of Photography*, 131
8. *Ansel Adams*, 9
9. *The Portfolios of Ansel Adams*, Introduction to *Portfolio Seven*
10. *The Portfolio of Ansel Adams*, Introduction to *Portfolio Three*
11. *Yosemite and the Range of Light*, 7
12. Ibid., 8
13. *Ansel Adams*, 21
14. *The Portfolios of Ansel Adams*, Introduction to *Portfolio One*
15. Ibid., Introduction to *Portfolio Four*

List of Plates

The photographs in this book were supplied by:

COVER *Kearsage Pinnacles*
Kings River Canyon, California
The National Archives

BACK
COVER *Grand Canyon National Park*
Grand Canyon National Park, Arizona
The National Archives

TITLE
PAGE *Ansel Adams*
The Bettman Archive
New York

PLATE 1 *In Glacier National Park*
Glacier National Park, Montana
The National Archives

PLATE 2 *Grand Teton*
Grand Teton National Park, Wyoming
The National Archives

PLATE 3 *Rocky Mountain National Park, Never Summer Range*
Rocky Mountain National Park, Colorado
The National Archives

PLATE 4 *Rock of Ages, Big Room, Carlsbad Caverns National Park*
Carlsbad Caverns National Park, New Mexico
The National Archives

PLATE 5 *Saguaros, Saguaro National Monument*
Saguaro National Monument, Arizona
The National Archives

PLATE 6 *From Logan Pass, Glacier National Park*
Glacier National Park, Montana
The National Archives

PLATE 7 *Grand Teton*
Grand Teton National Park, Wyoming
The National Archives

PLATE 8 *Grand Canyon National Park*
Grand Canyon National Park, Arizona
The National Archives